MATCAT

EXPLORING COUNTRIES

Nicaragua

by Lisa Owings

BELLWETHER MEDIA · MINNEAPOLIS, MN

Note to Librarians, Teachers, and Parents:

Blastoff! Readers are carefully developed by literacy experts and combine standards-based content with developmentally appropriate text.

Level 1 provides the most support through repetition of high-frequency words, light text, predictable sentence patterns, and strong visual support.

Level 2 offers early readers a bit more challenge through varied simple sentences, increased text load, and less repetition of high-frequency words.

Level 3 advances early-fluent readers toward fluency through increased text and concept load, less reliance on visuals, longer sentences, and more literary language.

Level 4 builds reading stamina by providing more text per page, increased use of punctuation, greater variation in sentence patterns, and increasingly challenging vocabulary.

Level 5 encourages children to move from "learning to read" to "reading to learn" by providing even more text, varied writing styles, and less familiar topics.

Whichever book is right for your reader, Blastoff! Readers are the perfect books to build confidence and encourage a love of reading that will last a lifetime!

This edition first published in 2015 by Bellwether Media, Inc.

No part of this publication may be reproduced in whole or in part without written permission of the publisher. For information regarding permission, write to Bellwether Media, Inc., Attention: Permissions Department, 5357 Penn Avenue South, Minneapolis, MN 55419.

Library of Congress Cataloging-in-Publication Data

Owings, Lisa.
  Nicaragua / by Lisa Owings.
     pages cm – (Blastoff! Readers: Exploring Countries)
  Summary: "Developed by literacy experts for students in grades three through seven, this book introduces young readers to the geography and culture of Nicaragua"– Provided by publisher.
  Audience: Ages 7-12.
  Includes bibliographical references and index.
  ISBN 978-1-60014-985-6 (hardcover : alk. paper)
  1. Nicaragua–Juvenile literature. I. Title.
  F1523.2.O85 2014
  972.85–dc 3

                                                                                    2014004677

Printed in the United States of America, North Mankato, MN.

Contents

Honduras

Nicaragua

Lake
Managua

Managua

Lake
Nicaragua

Pacific
Ocean

Caribbean
Sea

Costa Rica

N

W   E

S

Nicaragua is the largest country in Central America. It lies in the middle of the strip of land that connects North and South America. Nicaragua shares a long border with Honduras to the north. To the south is Costa Rica.

Central America stretches between two oceans. The turquoise waters of the Caribbean Sea bathe Nicaragua's eastern shores. Its western coast dips into the vast Pacific Ocean. Slightly **inland** from the Pacific coast are several large freshwater lakes. The country's capital and largest city, Managua, stands on the southern shore of Lake Managua.

Mountains cover much of west-central Nicaragua. The land reaches its highest point at Mogotón Peak, along the border with Honduras. Between the central mountains and the western coast lies Lake Nicaragua. This great lake is the largest in Central America. To its northwest is Lake Managua. A chain of **volcanoes** cuts through the lakes. Their smoking cones rise out of the **lowlands** that stretch to the western shore.

The **plains** east of the mountains are carpeted with **rain forests**. Rivers from the mountains wind through the forests on their way to the Caribbean Sea. Beaches dot the Caribbean coast. The eastern shoreline is fringed with small islands and **coral reefs**.

! fun fact

Nicaragua is warm year-round. The weather in the mountains is cooler. Most of the country's rain falls east of the mountains.

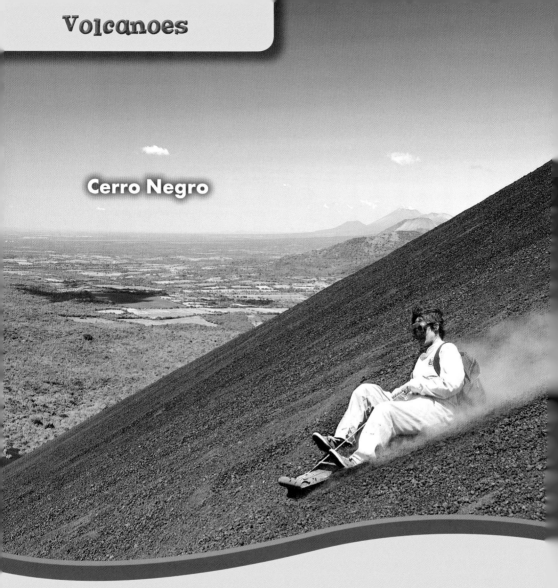

Cerro Negro

A chain of some 40 volcanoes stretches along Nicaragua's Pacific coast. Many of the volcanoes are still active. Momotombo is an active volcano famous for its beautiful shape. Its steep cone rises above Lake Managua. Cerro Negro is black and barren. Many people use boards to sled down its sandy slopes.

The slopes of Mombacho are covered in a rare **cloud forest**. People can hike the volcano's misty, fern-laced trails. San Cristóbal is the highest volcano in Nicaragua. It is also one of the most active. Clouds of ash and gas often pour from its **crater**. Only the most experienced hikers climb to the top of this fuming peak.

fun fact

The Masaya volcano spews toxic gas. Few living things can survive near its crater. However, a group of green parakeets lives inside the volcano!

Masaya volcano

bull shark

Wildlife thrives in Nicaragua. The rain forests are home to jaguars and ocelots. Howler monkeys sound their alarm from the trees. Parrots flit from branch to branch. The ground crawls with ants, beetles, and other insects. Anteaters snatch them up for a meal with their long, sticky tongues.

ocelot

anteater

leatherback
sea turtle

fun fact

Named for their soft shells, leatherbacks are the largest turtles in the world. These gentle giants can weigh up to 2,000 pounds (900 kilograms)!

In the mountains, sly pumas stalk white-tailed deer. Hawks circle above Lake Nicaragua, while herons and egrets stand over its surface. At night, sea turtles nest on sandy beaches along the coasts. Rare hawksbill and leatherback sea turtles are among those found in Nicaraguan waters.

Around 6 million people live in Nicaragua. Most have homes in the western part of the country. The majority of Nicaraguans come from a mix of **native** and European **ancestors**. These people are called *mestizos*. Less than two out of every ten Nicaraguans have only Spanish or other European ancestors. Very few have only native ancestors.

Native Nicaraguans in the eastern forests speak their own languages. They live much as they did long ago. A small number of Nicaraguans with African and Caribbean ancestors have kept their culture alive in the east. Nearly all Nicaraguans speak Spanish, the country's official language.

Speak Spanish!

English	Spanish	How to say it
hello	hola	OH-lah
good-bye	adiós	ah-dee-OHS
yes	sí	SEE
no	no	NOH
please	por favor	POHR fah-VOR
thank you	gracias	GRAH-see-uhs
friend (male)	amigo	ah-MEE-goh
friend (female)	amiga	ah-MEE-gah

Family comes first for Nicaraguans. Most **rural** children have several brothers and sisters. They live with their extended family all in one home. In the countryside, children spend a lot of time doing chores. They might also work to earn money for the family. Children in cities usually have more time to play.

To get around, Nicaraguans in cities drive cars or ride buses. However, many roads in Nicaragua are too damaged to drive on. Some places can only be reached by special vehicles or horses. Nicaraguans shop at malls, supermarkets, or neighborhood stores called *pulperías*. Many people buy groceries from fruit trucks or sellers that go door to door.

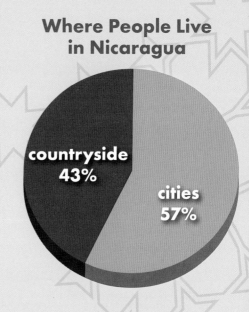

Where People Live in Nicaragua

countryside 43%

cities 57%

Schools in Nicaragua have improved greatly in the past few decades. However, students in the country still face many challenges. Most Nicaraguans start first grade at age 6. Yet only about half are able to finish sixth grade. Many cannot afford school supplies. Some children have to leave school to help support their families. In the countryside, schools are often far away or do not offer classes beyond fourth grade.

Students who do continue in school learn math, science, reading, and writing. Classes are taught in Spanish. After twelve years of school, Nicaraguans who can afford college may apply to universities. Many wealthy families send their children to college overseas.

Did you know?

Before 1980, fewer than half of Nicaraguans could read. The government made a huge effort to change that number. Now, about eight out of every ten Nicaraguans can read and write.

Where People Work in Nicaragua

manufacturing 19%

services 53%

farming 28%

Farming is a way of life for about one out of every three Nicaraguans. On the country's **fertile** western plains, farmers grow rice, beans, corn, and bananas. Coffee beans are grown in the mountains. Many farmers also raise cattle. Off the coasts, people fish for shrimp and lobster. Some Nicaraguans dig for gold. Factory workers in cities make food products, clothing, and fuel to sell to other countries.

About half of Nicaraguans have **service jobs**. Many sell goods in shops or markets. Teachers and doctors work to improve the country's schools and hospitals. Nicaraguans who work in hotels and restaurants make sure **tourists** enjoy their stay.

Nicaraguans are crazy about baseball. After school, children meet their friends at parks or in the streets for a game. They often use sticks for bats and rolled up cloth for balls. Fans also gather at baseball fields or around televisions sets to cheer on their favorite teams. Soccer and basketball are other popular sports.

Families often take day trips to the beach. People love to swim, surf, and relax in the warm sun. Trails through the country's mountains and forests are perfect for hiking or horseback riding. In the evenings, Nicaraguans enjoy going dancing with friends. Even children often stay out late into the night.

fun fact

Nicaraguans often pass the time by listening to street musicians play marimbas, guitars, and other instruments.

Nicaraguans enjoy simple but flavorful food. The most popular dish is *gallo pinto*, or beans and rice. Many Nicaraguans eat *gallo pinto* daily. Corn is another popular Nicaraguan food. In *nacatamales*, corn dough is stuffed with meat and cooked in **plantain** leaves. Fried plantains are a popular side dish.

Lunch is the biggest meal of the day. Many Nicaraguans come home from work or school to eat with their families. Salad and grilled meat often accompany beans and rice. Soups are also common. Soup made with vegetables and cow's stomach is called *sopa de mondongo*. For dessert, Nicaraguans eat *tres leches* cake. It is flavored with three kinds of milk. Tropical fruits also sweeten a meal.

pinolillo

gallo pinto

fun fact

Pinolillo is a popular drink made from cornmeal and cocoa. Nicaraguans like it so much that *pinoleros*, or *pinolillo* makers, is a common nickname for them.

Did you know?
For several weeks before Easter, many Nicaraguans do not eat red meat. Instead, they eat iguana meat or seafood.

Easter

24

Holidays in Nicaragua are often religious. The most important holiday is *Purísima*. This Christian celebration in December honors the Virgin Mary. Families decorate **altars** on their porches. They also celebrate with music, firecrackers, and parades. *Gritería* is part of *Purísima*. On December 7, children go from door to door. They ask, "Who brings us so much happiness?" Then they receive the answer, "The Virgin Mary!" along with a bag of treats.

Each Nicaraguan city holds a festival to celebrate its **patron saint**. These festivals include parades, dances, and sometimes **bullfights**. In September, Nicaragua celebrates its independence from Spain. The best students in Nicaragua pass a torch from border to border, and bands march through the streets.

In the 1600s, pirates took shelter along Nicaragua's Caribbean coast. They hid on the islands and planned their attacks on Spanish **settlers**. The **notorious** Captain Henry Morgan and others sailed up the San Juan River. They crossed Lake Nicaragua to attack the wealthy city of Granada and steal its gold. The Spanish had to build a **fortress** over the river to keep the pirates out.

Pirates also did some good in Nicaragua. They founded more towns than they attacked. Bluefields, Pueblo Viejo, and several other towns began as pirate hideouts. Nicaraguans still speak excitedly about sunken ships and buried treasure. These pirate **legends** are one way they keep their country's history alive.

Henry Morgan

Fast Facts About Nicaragua

Nicaragua's Flag

Nicaragua's flag has three horizontal bands of blue, white, and blue. The colors represent the strip of land between the Pacific and the Caribbean. In the center of the flag is a coat of arms that stands for equality and freedom. The design goes back to the 1800s, when Central America won its independence. Nicaragua adopted this flag in 1908.

Official Name: Republic of Nicaragua

Area: 50,336 square miles (130,370 square kilometers); Nicaragua is the 98th largest country in the world.

Capital City:	Managua
Important Cities:	León, Masaya, Granada
Population:	5,788,531 (July 2013)
Official Language:	Spanish
National Holiday:	Independence Day (September 15)
Religions:	Christian (82.6%), other (1.7%), none (15.7%)
Major Industries:	farming, services, tourism
Natural Resources:	gold, silver, copper, timber, fish
Manufactured Products:	food products, clothing, fuel, chemicals, machinery
Farm Products:	coffee beans, sugarcane, rice, beans, corn, bananas, beef, shrimp
Unit of Money:	Nicaraguan córdoba; the córdoba is divided into 100 centavos.

Glossary

altars—tables or platforms used as a focus for worship

ancestors—relatives who lived long ago

bullfights—spectacles in which a person fights with a bull; in Nicaraguan bullfights, one person wears the bull down and another person tries to ride it.

cloud forest—a tropical mountain forest that is covered in clouds year-round

coral reefs—structures made of coral that usually grow in shallow seawater

crater—the mouth of a volcano

fertile—able to support growth

fortress—a building that protects against attacks

inland—located away from the sea

legends—stories from the past; legends are widely accepted but cannot be proven as fact.

lowlands—areas of land that are lower than their surroundings

native—originally from a specific place

notorious—well-known or famous for doing something bad

patron saint—a saint who is believed to look after a country or group of people

plains—large areas of flat land

plantain—a type of banana that is less sweet and is usually cooked

rain forests—thick, green forests that receive a lot of rain

rural—relating to the countryside

service jobs—jobs that perform tasks for people or businesses

settlers—people who go to live in a new place where no or few others live

tourists—people who travel to visit another place

volcanoes—holes in the earth; when a volcano erupts, hot ash, gas, or melted rock called lava shoots out.

To Learn More

AT THE LIBRARY
Hamilton, Sue. *Henry Morgan*. Edina, Minn.: ABDO
Pub. Co., 2007.

Shields, Charles J. *Nicaragua*. Broomall, Penn.:
Mason Crest Publishers, 2009.

Torres, John. *Meet Our New Student from
Nicaragua*. Hockessin, Del.: Mitchell Lane
Publishers, 2009.

ON THE WEB
Learning more about Nicaragua
is as easy as 1, 2, 3.

1. Go to www.factsurfer.com.

2. Enter "Nicaragua" into the search box.

3. Click the "Surf" button and you will see a list of
   related web sites.

With factsurfer.com, finding more information is just
a click away.

Index